LEARNING
to LET GO
and GROW

LEARNING
to LET GO
and GROW

100 More Messages for Growth and Healing

Lisa Flannigan, PhD

LUMINARE PRESS
WWW.LUMINAREPRESS.COM

Learning to Let Go and Grow
Copyright © 2020 Lisa Flannigan, PhD

All rights reserved. This book or any portion thereof may not be reproduced or used in any manner whatsoever without the express written permission of the publisher, except for the use of brief quotations in a book review.

Printed in the United States of America

Cover Design: Melissa K. Thomas

Luminare Press
442 Charnelton St.
Eugene, OR 97401
www.luminarepress.com

LCCN: 2020908659
ISBN: 978-1-64388-383-0

This book is dedicated to our enduring spirit in this surreal time as we navigate the COVID-19 world pandemic.

Acknowledgements

I AM SO GRATEFUL to many wonderful people who have contributed to my ability to keep writing.

First and foremost, my beloved husband, Kris. Thank you for being there all these years. I appreciate that you are there to offer your voice of reason when I need it. Thank you, Dad, Joseph Thoben, for being someone to talk to about life.

Thank you, Mom, Nancy Thoben, for encouraging the love of books and reading throughout my life.

As always, thank you to my children, their spouses, and my grandchildren: Nick and Courtney; Kelli and Justin; Emma, Ben, and Phoebe. You all make my life more meaningful and beautiful, and I am eternally grateful.

Thank you Anne Niggemeyer-Hall, my dear friend, for providing such compassionate support across the miles.

Thank you again to the fantastic publishing team at Luminare Press for your organized, efficient, and smooth process of making this book a reality. Especially Kim. You cannot imagine how helpful all the "handholding" was.

Again, I want to thank all of my clients, who continue to trust me with their experiences and emotions as they navigate their challenges, striving to find peace and joy in their lives. Thank you, readers of *Learning to Trust Yourself* for all the positive feedback through emails, letters, messages, and reviews. Your comments about your favorite messages and how they spoke to you were heartwarming and touched me deeply. Keep reaching out to me. I read everything thoughtfully.

Thank you, reader. You are the reason I continue to write and share. Keep working toward a more meaningful life journey.

Introduction

I have, once again, felt called to write a book sharing brief encouraging messages to support you on your life journey. I was inundated with positive feedback from my first book, *Learning to Trust Yourself*, and was asked for more of the same. So, I am responding to those requests.

This book is entitled *Learning to Let Go and Grow*. It addresses the challenges in letting go of the unhelpful behaviors and thoughts that entangle us, leaving little room for joy, love, and hope. I believe that as our focus shifts from what is not going well in our lives to what is good, dramatic positive change can occur. It is not easy to attend to the sunshine in the distance when it is raining buckets where you stand. I am just suggesting a slight shift and an openness to explore the possibility of light in your life. Even a slightly different perspective can create an opportunity to allow more love, light, and joy in your life where there was pain or despair.

I have and continue to struggle with my inner saboteur at times and do practice what I preach. I need to keep a dedicated space in my life for self-care through journaling, meditating, positive self-talk, music, exercise, and being in nature.

I hope that you enjoy these messages and find your own self-care rituals that work for you. As always, take what is helpful and meaningful to you in your life. I suggest only reading and reflecting on one message a day or week. Again, this book is not meant to be a substitute for appropriate mental health treatment. My hope is that it can augment your work with a mental health professional.

1

When you look at yourself in the mirror and focus only on flaws, you miss all of your attributes. You are not taking in the whole of your magnificent being. You have diminished yourself to only those parts of you that bother you. What if you greeted yourself with a warm smile and could see the glow that you radiate? See yourself with eyes of wonder and appreciation for all that you are. View yourself with eyes of love and acceptance. Amazingly, the flaws become charming and melt into the greater sparkling image of "You."

2

Sometimes you have to let problems simmer on the back-burner while you go about daily living. Trust that the answers will come. They are working themselves out by your awareness that they need resolutions. How this occurs is amazing. Just believe in yourself.

3

Meditation is the most crucial practice for self-growth. Having this space to calm your nervous system allows healing and positive energy to flow through you. It is the daily habit that is important; occasional meditating is helpful but will not provide the greatest benefit. Giving yourself this gift is one that will continue giving back to you and others in your life.

4

Some days you may feel weary and depleted yet required to show up and perform. Just be present as much as you can. You may move slower and feel the toll of every step. Even if it is challenging, try paying attention to what you are experiencing. Within that space there is a gift or a lesson. Do not miss it.

5

Feeling out of balance and obsessed with a project is not a fertile environment for positive growth. This frantic state can block productive energy. Taking a break by doing something else self-nurturing will allow the creative flow to come back naturally. Trust that by putting it aside temporarily, you can return to it with better insight.

6

There may be something that you want very much right now. Longing is uncomfortable but sometimes necessary to point you in a direction. As you begin to move in that direction, it will become clearer to you if it is truly what you desire or just a catalyst to get you moving toward a general goal. You will not know until you actually take careful steps toward it.

7

Sometimes you may be faced with a concern that needs resolution. There may be something you think is going to help, but it is difficult. However, it may be necessary. You may ruminate about moving forward because it feels right but is a hard choice. When you realize that it is the only option for your peace of mind, you will know it is the best decision for you.

8

You cannot be responsible for things that you do not have control over. You may be tempted to believe you can do something to make someone be, feel, or act differently. You do not have that power. People are responsible for their own choices even when it is difficult for you to watch them go through painful experiences. You are on your own path and can only be responsible for your own choices.

9

Protect your positive energy. Visualize a shield whenever you are around someone's negative energy. They may just be having a tough day, and you may want to lift their spirits. That is OK. However, sometimes people's negativity invades our peaceful space and permeates our mind, then spreads like a wildfire through us to someone else. You can transform that darkness into light by refusing to accept the negativity.

10

Sometimes people are cruel or hostile. It is about what is going on with them. It can be helpful to remind yourself that it is not about you. You are worthy of being treated with respect and care. Try not to allow their pain to become yours.

11

Putting yourself out there can be frightening. Knowing when to do so and when to tighten your boundaries and protect yourself is an art. It comes from getting acquainted with who you are and what you need. Then acknowledge what you have to offer that may be of value to others. This process can take time to master. Be patient with yourself.

12

Sometimes your mind goes to a dark place where you can only see yourself negatively. This can be torturous. Remember this will pass. You may be tired, stressed, or replaying old hurtful messages given to you when you were young and vulnerable. You do not have to believe them anymore. They were not the truth. You were always deserving of care and acceptance. Notice and acknowledge those painful feelings. Have compassion for yourself. Breathe deeply. Then let them go.

13

I am sorry that you sometimes feel so alone even among people that you care about. Is it that you are in a different emotional space than they are right now? We cannot always be in the same place at the same time. You can choose to take some time to comfort yourself as you process your emotions. Or you can ask someone you trust to enter that space with you. Feeling disconnected just happens sometimes. Even though it is not pleasant, it is often part of emotional growth.

14

Sometimes even when you have problems falling asleep, you just need to go to bed. Staying up obsessing is not going to bring you peace. Even if you have trouble winding down and your mind is full of racing thoughts, go through your evening ritual and lay down in a dark room on a comfortable bed. Give yourself this opportunity to rest. It will signal your brain it is time to settle down and let go of the day. Eventually your mind and body will get the message, and the rhythm of your sleep cycle will return.

15

Sometimes you may feel to blame for other people's actions or emotions. However, their behaviors and managing their feelings are under their control—not yours. It may be challenging to accept this truth. When you have carried those burdens in the past, they can be difficult to let go of. You may have been held accountable for things that were not yours. Although your behavior can impact other people, you are only responsible for your actions and emotions. As human beings, we have free will and choices. People are allowed to make bad decisions, and there is nothing you can do to change that.

16

Sometimes when you are feeling low it is good to realize that this is the time for self-nurturing. It is not a time to expect more from yourself, such as to "snap out of it" or will yourself to "be happy." It is a time for taking care of the part of you that needs extra care and support. You may need a walk, a nap, to journal, or to just comfort yourself in the best way for you. People may have expectations for you, but you need to advocate for yourself. Only you know what you need.

17

Feeling overwhelmed by too many demands can be devastating. Everything can feel like it is too much and that you do not have what is necessary to meet all those expectations of you. You may not be able to fulfill all of those requests for your time and attention. This is the time to seek help, guidance, and resources. You do not have to know it all or have all the answers. You can admit that you are human and may have to learn some things. Have faith in your capacity to learn, ask for help, and break down the rest into small manageable tasks that you can handle. Let go of the need to do it all perfectly. Accept where you are, and remember to breathe and take time out to clear you head. This part of your journey will not last forever. It is just an arduous hill.

18

Feeling guilty about having joy in your life when other people are suffering happens because you are human. Having compassion for others is a good thing. However, punishing yourself does not help other people. When you are comfortably able to share your resources with others, you can do so. It is important to remember that you cannot save everyone or fix them. Their struggle could be part of their process to healing and greater joy. You cannot rob them of their own self-discovery. You can send them loving thoughts. Most importantly, be grateful, not guilty, for what you enjoy.

19

Some days it may feel like everyone is against you. You may be defensive and ready to battle with anyone as a result. It is hard, but let go of the need to prove yourself right and another wrong. It is appropriate to be assertive and stand up for yourself. However, it is better received coming from a place of respect. Misunderstandings that get amplified with hostility or sarcasm do not lead to peaceful resolutions for anyone.

20

When you need to end a relationship with someone because it is not working out for either of you, you may feel sad or guilty for a little while. It is hard to let people know you no longer want them in your life. You may feel anguish over the pain your rejection may cause them. For closure, it can be helpful to thank them for what you appreciated about them and to take responsibility for your role in what did not work. It is your life and your choice. You cannot stay in a relationship of any kind that hurts your soul and does not enhance either of your lives. As painful as it is, you are doing what is healthy for you.

21

Adapting to changes in your life can be challenging. It takes time getting used to something new and different. Be patient with yourself. It can be frightening when things are unfamiliar. Over time you will begin to feel more comfortable. As you accommodate the changes in your life, you will develop a renewed sense of security.

22

When you have a tough decision to make, try to believe it will be resolved for the best outcome for you and all involved. Sometimes it may feel like a choice between what is right for you and what is right for someone else. If it is truly right for you, then it will be the best for the others involved as well because it is the honest choice. Make the decision that brings you the greatest peace. Unfortunately, there may be those that will not see it that way and may be upset with you. Trust yourself in this thoughtful process. If at any time it does not seem to be the best option, then you can change your mind. It is never too late to renegotiate what is right for you.

23

Being afraid of the unknown is about not trusting yourself. You have come through many challenges successfully. Some may not have been fun, but you grew from each experience. You will continue to do so. You can rely on your strength. Spending time imagining the worst creates more fear and negativity. Try affirming and enjoying all that is going well and believe it will continue.

24

Engaging in joy-filled behavior every day lightens your load. When your heart is allowed to enjoy and play, your life will grow brighter and shine. Find what brings you joy. Focus on that. Allow your struggles to diminish in magnitude. Your challenges may still be there but will not stay center stage.

25

Treat people with respect, empathy, and value—whether they deserve it or not. This is a higher level of communication. Although we all regress at times, striving to honor another person's humanity makes us all better people.

26

Allow time in your life to discover your creativity. It does not matter what form you engage in. Do not judge critically what you create. Give yourself that space. To express yourself is healing and balancing. When you create something, you share a piece of yourself with the world. It is an incredible feeling to give birth to that energy.

27

Talk to yourself with love and compassion. You are the best friend you will ever have. Develop an internal voice that is encouraging, supportive, and kind. You can rely on that support when life feels cruel.

28

Some days you may feel like your life is a mess. It is hard to see the order and pattern when you are inspecting it too closely. Take a step back. Close your eyes. Breathe. Ground yourself. Trust that the mess you think you see is an emerging change. When you are in a transition, things seem in disarray. The old and unhelpful is being remodeled into something more useful. Be patient. It will all fall into place perfectly for you.

29

Taking care of yourself is not always glamorous. Going to the doctor or dentist when you need to, eating nutritious food, exercising, or making sure that your bills are paid on time are all important ways to care for yourself. If you can change the way you see these tasks, they will seem less daunting. Try to remember that providing nurturing care for yourself keeps you happy and healthy. Be grateful that you have money to pay your bills, healthcare, access to nutrient-rich foods, and a strong body to take care of.

30

Try to remind yourself that you are doing enough and what you have already accomplished is good. Being here in this moment is enough. You do not always have to work at doing more and more to earn your value as a worthwhile person. Know when it is enough for now.

31

Remaining grateful, letting go, and having faith are superpowers in times of stress. They will help you refocus your energy where it is the most effective.

32

Take gentle care of yourself, and keep safe boundaries. You know where you are vulnerable. Help others only as much as it does not hurt you.

33

You are entitled to set healthy boundaries for yourself. Just because someone demands your attention does not mean that you have to engage them. Even those of us with compassionate hearts deserve to create a safe space around ourselves. Someone else's crisis is not ours to manage. Being available to others in the way you choose is your right. You can have firm boundaries and still be a caring person.

34

Fatigue or illness is often a message to slow down and be present. Rushing through your day avoiding experiencing each moment fully causes you to miss so much. When this day is over, it is history. Relish the mundane tasks even if you do them every day. This is your life. Embrace it so when you look back you do not yearn for what you left behind.

35

It can be easy to become distracted from how you want to use your gifts in this world. When you find yourself caught up in the chaos of activity and realize that you are not focused on what you want to create, it is helpful to take a moment. Close your eyes, breathe, and listen. Ask yourself: How do I want to feel instead? Focus on the desired feeling. Then decide the best course of action for that outcome.

36

Please try to avoid becoming infected by people's uncomfortable energy. Guard your sacred space. Gently guide them to an awareness of their own light or move away if they are unable to make the shift. Forgive yourself if you temporarily get lost in the murkiness. Return to your center and move on.

37

If you wait too long to check in with yourself, it may be harder to find you again. Avoid losing yourself to others' demands. Staying engaged and connected with people who are important to you is healthy. However, balance the socializing with quiet time alone for self-reflection or with creative expression. Connecting with yourself soothes an inner aching that cannot be met by anyone else.

38

Slow down and pay attention. When you are fully present, you cannot also be overwhelmed. By breathing and resting in the space between thoughts and actions, you may be able to accomplish more. In that grounded space, you can face a day with many demands. It can be your source of calm within a storm.

39

When someone you care about shares their pain with you, it is hard to resist the urge to fix it for them. Unfortunately, you cannot take away their pain. Let them know that you care and are sorry they are hurting. Ask them if they need you to just listen, or if there is another way you can support them? Then, although it may be difficult, you will need to let go. Allow them to grow through their pain in their own way.

40

Listening to that inner voice that guides you to peaceful acceptance can be challenging at times. To hear it, you must quiet the static and distracting chatter in your mind. Breathe. Let go. And trust that your inner guidance is there for you deep inside beneath the fear and loud outer noise.

41

Sometimes you may feel like a different person than the one looking back at you in the mirror. Feeling disconnected from your physical image can be alarming. You may not be feeling attuned to what you see. That is because inside of you there can be many different emotional states. The outside may not always match up with how you feel inside. Just love and accept all of the different parts of you, whether they are in sync or not. As you grow emotionally, you will feel whole more often.

42

When you are feeling overwhelmed by demands and overtired or unwell, it is important to first take care of yourself physically. Pushing through and neglecting your needs will not increase your productivity. When you take time to acknowledge how you are feeling and what you need, you will have the capacity to move forward with projects. It can be annoying to have to stop and listen to your body. However, the best work comes when you are strong, healthy, and centered. Be compassionate with yourself, and take care of your body.

43

When it happens again—that lonely sinking feeling—remind yourself that it is temporary. Those feelings are not the truth of who you are. Compassion heals emotional pain. Speak reassuringly to yourself, practice a self-soothing activity like listening to music, taking a bath, writing in a journal, or taking a walk. You will get through this dark time. Just rest and seek comfort. Tomorrow will be filled with hope.

44

Feeling devalued, left out, or unimportant are crushing experiences. However, they are only feelings. You are important and worthy of being included, whether you feel that way or not. Emotions do not determine your value. They do not define the complexity of who you are. Some are unpleasant, but they cannot make you less deserving of love and belonging.

45

Being human makes you vulnerable to having desires, distractions, emotions, and needs. Sometimes, unfortunately, all of them may conflict with one another. Trying to settle into a peaceful place of knowing how to prioritize these opposing demands of your time and attention can be challenging. Taking time each day to be still and open to inner guidance can help you organize internal chaos.

46

Being able to use and share your unique gifts with others is pure joy. Discover the interests, talents, and skills you possess that bring you happiness when you express them. You have special abilities that are unique to you. You may or may not be aware of them or acknowledge them, but they exist. Allowing this intricate blueprint within you to unfold is magical. Expressing it offers something of value to others while you enjoy being in your creative zone.

47

Sometimes heartbreaking news can make you feel helpless. It is challenging to keep an open heart and to hope for the healing of our world. Seeing the light in so much darkness may seem impossible. Focus on the comforting peace within you that we all share—not the darkness. Send your loving energy to those who need it while staying grounded in your sacred center.

48

It can be tenuous sometimes to remember your value when you are feeling like a burden or not worthwhile. There may be a fragile sense of yourself offering something to others. This thin thread can be built upon until you regain a sense of your own worth. Do not lose it. Hold on carefully. It is there as always, deep within, as strong and vibrant as ever.

49

Our emotions can be fickle and unpredictable sometimes. One day we may feel as though our world is over as we crash into deep despair. The very next day, one event may cause a shift and we feel joy and gratitude. It is important to avoid pouring gasoline on that spark of negative emotion. Allow yourself to feel and express yourself if you need to. However, ruminating over painful emotions with aggressive thoughts against yourself or someone else is like fanning that fire, and it can quickly burn out of control. Instead, soothe your pain with the image of cool water calming the flame.

50

Creating a peaceful haven inside helps you navigate unsettling situations. It provides you an inner compass that will consistently guide you toward the best outcome. Although it may require daily practice and commitment, the benefits are immeasurable. Seek peace first.

51

The urge to do more—to overanalyze or hover over your conflicts, trying to control them—is not productive. The best problem-solving comes from a relaxed mind and body. When you are able to clearly understand your dilemma, release your attachment to it, and the resolution will effortlessly emerge. Trust this process.

52

Negotiating the conflict between your desires and your emotions is an ongoing challenge. For example, you may desire peace but are excited about a new adventure. Both can be pleasant, but one seems to contradict the other. How to integrate both into your experience is an art. The key is to focus on the present moment. Being mindful of what you are feeling right now is where your power is.

53

This moment is where your peace is. Close your eyes and let go of everything else but the rhythm of your breath. Sink into the awareness that nothing matters but this sacred center of your being. All your problems, worries, and insecurities melt into the abyss. They are not important. You are. In this perfect comforting space, everything is OK. You are safe and loved.

54

When you are transitioning to a higher level of being, there may be discomfort. These growing pains will lessen as you become accustomed to flying with your new wings. Soon you will soar, and the awkwardness will dissipate.

55

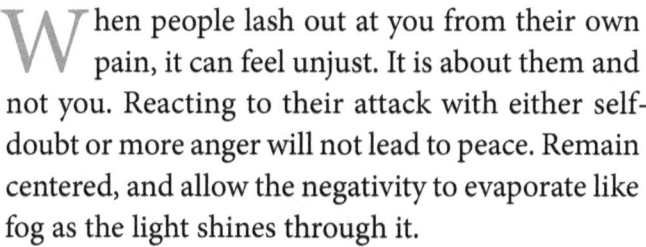

When people lash out at you from their own pain, it can feel unjust. It is about them and not you. Reacting to their attack with either self-doubt or more anger will not lead to peace. Remain centered, and allow the negativity to evaporate like fog as the light shines through it.

56

Sometimes tragic experiences pull us into a saddened space. We may feel deeply wounded and have a challenging time remaining hopeful about the future. Soothe yourself in the best way for you. Grief and vulnerability are an aspect of our human condition and can feel intolerable. When you are able to feel more steady, listen for that glimmer of hope. There may be a positive message underneath the pain.

57

Why is it so challenging to take time for yourself to be self-reflective? Is it because you do not want to know what your inner voice is telling you? Listening beyond those self-critical thoughts, judgements, and disappointments to the quiet presence underneath takes patience and practice. It is only here that you can experience your true essence, a beautiful creative being.

58

Feeling disconnected from a loving presence in your life happens when you do not acknowledge yourself. Being there for yourself helps you stay centered and grounded. Nothing can derail you when you have this solid foundation. Try to seek guidance from within instead of searching for an outer resource. You have everything you need.

59

Moving forward with your life happens like a dance—two steps forward, then a step back, and a few to the side. The momentum is toward your goals, dreams, and aspirations if you allow the ebb and flow of life to unfold. Where you are right now is the goal and the journey. Enjoy your dance.

60

You are so much more than what you see in the mirror. You have all that you need to create your beautiful life. Doubting yourself is temporary. You will remember who you are and what you are capable of.

61

Sometimes you may falter and feel weary. This is only a brief moment in your journey. Do not believe it is your destiny. It is merely an experience to strengthen your faith in yourself and to illuminate where you desire to be instead. Keep returning to the guiding light of your sacred center, and your struggles will melt away as if they never existed.

62

Removing your blocks to happiness in life is more important than attempting to acquire something outside yourself. Just like with learning to swim: Once you relax and experience your buoyancy, it is effortless. The realization that the water supports you when you let go is the magical moment you become a swimmer. This process is in your mind. Once you feel this, you no longer fight the fear of sinking and can enjoy the sensation of weightlessness. As in life, submersing in the ease of each moment extinguishes the blocks to enjoyment.

63

When will you know that you are doing enough? When will you experience the connection to your soul that guides you to your highest self? You are already doing enough. You are always connected to your most enlightened self. Instead of searching or doing more, try allowing and listening to the quiet presence within. When your mind is still, your internal compass is realigned. Trust it will guide you in the right direction.

64

Sometimes other people want *your* peace, joy, love, or happiness for themselves. They may crave it so desperately because of what is missing in them that they become aggressive and demanding. They may want the life that you created. All you can do is keep safe boundaries. You cannot lose your peace to rescue them. They need to learn for themselves what brings them happiness.

65

Create a sacred boundary around yourself that allows you to enjoy connection with others yet filters out harsh painful energy. Creativity, compassion, and joy happen when you are living in this space. Building a peaceful reflective center takes time, attention, and patience. However, it is worth the devotion and commitment.

66

When something within you is out of balance—whether it is your body fighting an illness or your mind needing to work through some dilemma or you are just feeling off—take time to rest. Trust that you will come back into homeostasis if you take that time. Gentleness with yourself in times of stress provides more enduring positive results than pushing past your limits. As a pendulum swings back and forth between extremes, it eventually settles in the center. You too will find your way back to your center if you allow this natural process of rebalancing.

67

Believing in yourself may be challenging at times. If you fixate on all the reasons that you are not capable, knowledgeable, or strong enough to move ahead with your dream, you will convince yourself it is unattainable. If, instead, you focus on what you would like to see happen, you will be able to chart a course toward one small reasonable goal and then another.

68

Some days when you attempt to be quiet and reflective, you may not feel centered or connected to your inner guidance. In these times it is important to let go of trying to force things. Relax and be present with your breathing. The lesson for you may be about letting go and trusting the moment.

69

When you are having one of those days that everything seems to overwhelm you, try to reassure yourself that this day is not going to last, but you will. Remember to allow those feelings to move through you on their way out. Do not get caught up in them or overanalyze. Just release and hold on to that place inside that is soothing, safe, and has hope.

70

Life can be so engaging and exciting sometimes. Afterwards, it can be challenging to regain your footing and ground yourself. Harmony is living in that perfect balance between joyful activity and quiet reflection.

71

Having racing thoughts swirl around in your mind can be frustrating. Which ones are important? Which ones should you ignore? A valuable tool to calm your thoughts and ease your mind is through a daily practice of mindful breathing and meditation. This habit helps you let go of your thoughts briefly as you focus on your breath and/or a mantra. With more clarity, you can begin to differentiate between those thoughts that are helpful and those that are not.

72

When your body is fighting off an illness, it can be unpleasant. It can be easy to believe that you are helpless, weak, alone, or even to become angry and blame yourself for getting sick. It is more helpful to rest and remember that your body is amazing and resourceful. It can restore itself to homeostasis while you take gentle care of it and remain grateful for this time to practice self-compassion.

73

Distractions in life are inevitable. How do you let go of fighting them and trust that you will regain your center? The answer is in the daily practice of allowing—remembering to let go of the thoughts that are not peaceful and loving and to focus only on that quiet inner knowing.

74

When you are not feeling self-assured and confident, try to accept help. Close your eyes, breathe deeply, and allow your inner guidance to come for you. You are not alone. You are loved and supported when you feel it and also when you cannot.

75

When painful emotions interfere with your peace of mind, release your need for them. Open your heart to choosing love instead. In that powerful shift, you will be free of the shackles of negative energy and able to allow unlimited positive flow instead.

76

When the hills in your life seem too steep to climb, stop and survey your landscape. Remember where you were and how far you have come. Every step forward is fueled by the lessons you have learned along the way. You used to crawl, but now you walk. You move gracefully through life, one adventure after another. This hill is not as challenging as you have imagined. So, proceed and relish the beautiful scenery along the way.

77

Letting go of old, unhelpful behaviors and beliefs can be difficult. Simply focus on adding positive thoughts and perspectives. As you grow and learn more useful coping patterns, the unhealthy ones will wither away from lack of use.

78

When you have a conflict with someone close to you, it can be painful and overwhelming. Trying to navigate self-expression and self-preservation with concern for the relationship is a delicate dance. Trust that communicating with respect will honor both of you. Repair damage to the relationship if emotions turn volatile. Taking space to cool down during intense emotions helps when discussing sensitive topics.

79

Search inside for a safe haven when there is a lot going on around you and in your mind and body. Trust that peaceful space is there. You only need to commit to allowing it to surface and feel the connection. Make the time to experience this each day, and every day in every way your life will get better.

80

Release the blocks in you that interfere with experiencing your value in this world. You are a unique expression of light that cannot be replicated. Feel this. Know it, and shine for all to benefit from your glow.

81

Guilt about taking care of yourself when other people believe you should be there for them is an uncomfortable dilemma. You cannot be helpful or available to anyone if you do not love and care for yourself. Feeling that you should always put others first is an impossible constraint you have placed on yourself. Attending to your needs allows you the space to be there for others. It guarantees that you are equipped to give and are not just making an empty gesture.

82

Accepting what gifts you are given and working with them in the most joyful way ensures they will multiply. What you may not believe is good enough is actually an amazing expression of you that nobody else can replicate. Please stop trying to be someone else. Just being you is more than enough.

83

What you see in others is inside of you. When you are disturbed by something dark and unpleasant in another person, it is often a lesson to forgive that part of yourself that you struggle to accept. Other people in our lives reflect what needs to be healed within us. Choosing to forgive what they mirror in us allows us to experience peace.

84

Continuing to believe in your dreams even when they do not turn out the way you had hoped can be challenging. It may be time to accept where you are and appreciate the life you have created so far. When you let go of the struggle, something better emerges seemingly from out of nowhere.

85

Focusing on your flaws will make them appear greater than they are. However, paying attention to your strengths will allow you to build more. Why is it so difficult to accept the good within? Why does any positive seem fleeting, and you search outside yourself—striving to be more, do better, or gain something? Your value resides inside of you. You cannot find it out there. Stay present, and acknowledge what is within.

86

When something irritates you and feels intolerable, do not resist it or fight it. This may seem counterintuitive. However, release your preconceived ideas about the irritant, and observe without judgement or intention to control it. Your acceptance will allow it to flow through you. If you learned something valuable, be grateful, and enjoy your restored peace.

87

When you are not feeling well, life's challenges can seem unbearable. Your perception is based on your present experience and may not be the most trustworthy evaluation. Give yourself some time and space to rest, heal, and re-evaluate your situation when you are feeling more grounded. Your options and choices will seem clearer and brighter if you take that space for yourself.

88

Your way in life may seem different and unpopular. Feeling out of sync with those around you who appear to be sailing through without obstacles is an illusion. Everyone has their challenges. You can only live your life for you. Feeling connected to others who understand you will happen when you are living authentically.

89

Connecting to the harmonious flow of the universe feels indescribable. It can happen spontaneously when you are taking in a beautiful sunset. It can also occur when you choose to forgive someone and let go of the injustice you have held onto. When you are in that blissful space, nothing else matters. Seeking it can only come by releasing attachment to outcomes and trusting it is there.

90

Sometimes the most meaningful and breathtaking experiences come after the most challenging. They are not related. You do not have to go through pain to feel good. It is only your focus on the joy in stark contrast to earlier discouragement that appears to connect them.

91

Instead of striving to do more, try doing less with more focus. Attention to the present moment in whatever you are doing is the most effective. Uncovering the drive behind constant unfocused activity can help you understand and release that tension. Find peace in whatever activity you are engaged in, and you will accomplish more.

92

Releasing resentments, disappointments, and expectations of others can be challenging. It is human nature to want to hold on to these barriers to intimacy to shield ourselves from perceived hurt. However, when we can let go of feeling wounded by another, we can experience healing within ourselves.

93

Close your eyes and empty all of your thoughts, worries, and mental occupations a few times a day. Just let go for a few moments. Allow healing energy to flow through your body. Experience the peace, and ride the wave of release with each breath. This is what being alive and conscious feels like. Enjoy.

94

It is easy to get caught up chasing what you do not want or need in your life. Being bombarded by flashy media images can tempt you to crave something you may believe will make you happy. Unfortunately, self-satisfaction and happiness can only come from within. Spending time being quiet and self-reflective helps you have some immunity to distracting messages.

95

How do you enjoy the life you have created when others are suffering? You may feel that you do not deserve your gifts because others may not have the resources you do. Blocking your joy does not help others. Enjoying and sharing your abundance is good. However, sometimes people are not able or ready to see or receive the love that is all around them. You cannot change their perceptions. You can be grateful and offer your light but cannot force their receiving it.

96

Just because right now you cannot see the way forward does not mean it is not there. It may just be obscured by shadows. Sometimes the only way to know the next step is to release what you do not want. Letting go of negative energy allows the path to emerge clearly before you.

97

When you are devastated by tragic news that will change your life, it can be destabilizing. Allow your emotions without judgement. They will cleanse you. Try to stay out of your fearful thoughts; they will not take you to a good place. Stay present and ride out the storm. Intense weather does not last forever. Comfort yourself in the best way for you, and trust in the light within you to be your guide. It will be alright even if it does not feel that way now.

98

When life feels too much, take time to rest and nurture yourself. Feel uncomfortable emotions, and soothe yourself with gentle care. It is not helpful to overthink when you are feeling fragile. Just allow and breathe. Focus on loving yourself through your pain. It is not there to remind you that you are not enough. It is there to remind you of the beautiful strength in your vulnerability. With self-compassion comes healing.

99

Loving yourself and allowing your inner light to shine is enough. When you bathe yourself in this powerful experience, you realize there is nothing else more important. This space is pure unlimited peace. All obstacles, concerns, and fears are dissolved. There is a sense of wholeness and connection to infinite possibilities. Everything else is trivial and meaningless. This is your most valuable asset.

100

You are on the right path for you. Even when it seems rocky and treacherous. Even when you are taking cautious deliberate steps. Even if you need to let go of extra baggage to lighten your load. Even when you are distracted and feel off track. Be confident that where you are right now is perfect. So, breathe, savor each moment, and enjoy your journey.

I hope that this book has been helpful to you in some way. If so, I would greatly appreciate your feedback, comments, and reviews on Amazon, Barnes and Noble, or on Instagram at drlisaflann. Or email me at lisaflannigan@gmail.com. Thank you.

www.ingramcontent.com/pod-product-compliance
Lightning Source LLC
LaVergne TN
LVHW091600060526
838200LV00036B/935